SUCK SUMMER SWEET

By
Jasmine Christi

2019

For Jon
and corner shop piss vodka

TOO SICKLY A SCENT

'In Petushki
the jasmine never stops blooming
and the birds always sing'

I worry you find jasmine too sickly a scent
And the blossom a burden
Sweeping it every morning
The birds were too loud
And of course out of tune

So you decided Petushki wasn't for you

GIVING UP ROMANTICISM

I gave up on Romanticism
After I realised
To love someone
You had to endure

Two week old towels
Overflowing laundry baskets
Off white bed sheets
Shirts with sweat stains
Ironing piles
Wet socks on the radiator

Laundry is a real romance killer

TUESDAYS

He played football every Tuesday night
His clothes were always soaked in either

Sweat

Rain

Blood

Mud

And this November night
It was all four

A pile of clothes dumped on my kitchen floor
The bath running

A 6ft man
In a 5ft bath

Shivering

I climbed in

I took the tap end

I dipped a finger in a scabby wound on his knee

I slid a line of blood across each cheek

I stuck my tongue out at him

And scrubbed his scabs clean

TUBE WINDOW

I've watched my face age
In the reflection of the window opposite me
On the tube
For 40 years

I no longer look up
I don't care to see my reflection

But I look up now
I can watch your reflection beside mine
And tell myself
I did alright
I deserve you

THE HEART OF A HOME

The heart of a home

Instead of
Pots
Pans
Smells

My kitchen contains
Empties
Bullets
And men

So you've heard of an AK-47

Yeah I've heard of an AK-47

This is a bullet from it

You wouldn't have stood a chance against that

I top up everyone's drinks
And tell the boys to put the war stuff
Back in the kitchen drawer

THE ALPHABETICAL LOVE LETTER

SUCK SUMMER SWEET

a, a, a, a, a, a, actions, aged, and, and, and, and,
and, anywhere, approach, body, both, claim, club,
convincing, cool, could, covered, cum, cum, cum,
drank, drunk, everywhere, face, face, face,
faulting, first, for, for, for, for, fuck, good, good,
had, had, hard, hold, hotel, I, I, I, I, I, I, I, I, if, in,
in, in, Jasmine, job, kiss, liked, liked, little, lips,
me, me, me, me, me, me, met, monk, movie,
much, my, my, my, my, my, my, myself, not, not,
of, off, on, or, pissed, pretty, remember, room,
room, scummy, so, spit, spit, spit, spit, spit,
straight, suck, summer, sweet, sweet, take, tastes,
tell, the, the, this, though, to, to, too, too, too,
want, was, was, was, went, were, were, you, you,
you, you, you, you, your

THE LOW

The good looking people eating with good looking
people
And the drunks drinking with the drunks

Me
Watching the glasses lined up on the bar
Deciding who to spend the night with

Only the drunks and the insane walk at this hour
Often they merge
Walking to homes and hobbies

I count myself amongst the latter

Getting a degree would be a better waste of time
Than working in a bar
Everyone working in bars thinks they have
something more going on
Bad habits they confuse with hobbies

One bottle left in the fridge
I think of how the whole community comes
together to empty the fridge

ANOTHER

More curtains
More men
More bodies
More pissers

Same towels
Same cigarettes
Same bed linen
Same wine

All this lovemaking is so comfortable
They even make me dinner sometimes

FAME

I only mess around with him because he knows
people

But he says those people are obsessed with other
people
And spend all their time trying to impress other
people
And he found out the people are only worried
about other people
And he wrote about the people

And lies in bed with the people

Writing to me

PIGEON

I have lived amongst pigeons for all my existence
Yet only twice has a pigeon ever inspired me to
write

There was a pigeon limping through Liverpool
Street station
Without a care for anyone

And then the beige pigeon outside King's Cross

Train pigeons are more cultured than the rest

Anyway
She was a burnt pink beige that faded into white
Her feathers were that of colours I had dreamt of
in southern European cities
Faded rusty clay walls warmed by the summer
heat
Clay pots waiting to be glazed
Fingerprints after being dabbed with face makeup

A pigeon brought more inspiration to me than anyone standing on the train platform

GROCERY LIST

What do you need from the store?

Milk

Eggs

Birth Control

Milk

Eggs

Birth Control

I never buy any of those things

TINDER DATE OUTSIDE THE ELGIN

Yeah you're pretty, not traffic-stopping, but why
would you need to be?
I don't know if your writing is any good, I'm sure it
is, but there we go
Might have a fag

Go on, have a fag, I've still got half my gin

I once went all the way to Leicester for a Tinder
date

Did you get the train to Leicester?

Yeah I got the train to Leicester
Met this cute broad
Sitting at a pub, a bit like this, we were drinking,
laughing, and you know, I go for a piss
All good, come back, the chick's gone
She left half a glass of gin

She got up and left?
Didn't even finish her gin?

I need a piss and looking at your half glass is
making me nervous

Go piss babe, I wouldn't leave a drink

07:12 TRAIN KING'S X -> ELY

I'm home now
Curled up against the radiator

How does it compare to me?

Incomparable

Bet the radiator doesn't snore

And needs less maintenance

I'll be your radiator

If you'll be my two bar heater

I run on gas but you're electric

SKY OF HANGOVER

From 4 pm to 4 am we are the most productive

I still haven't become acclimatised to London by
night
The night is never as dark as I remembered
The night is always a grotesque shade of yellow
Resembling the synaesthetic colour of a hangover

Maybe these ugly skies fuel the work
Work through the hangover
And demand less from a sunrise

ANSWER YOUR FUCKING PHONE

Today there were no meaningful words exchanged

No inspiration came

You called and I missed it
And I called
And you missed it

We couldn't make it today

When you're not around
It leaves me little to write about

I'll call again tomorrow

IKEA REVOLUTION

After weeks of watching his movements and habits
I reached the conclusion
That he did nothing intentionally

Events naturally materialised
Or didn't

E.g. three chests of drawers awaiting assembly in
the hallway

He had a theory about the Ikea revolution
People secretly like the construction element
It's rewarding work in this dynamic
You move the construction element to the
consumer

We did not enjoy the construction element

Hey babe, let's hit a new relationship milestone, let's assemble furniture together

Three chests of drawers remain in the hallway

I DIDN'T HAVE A CLASSICAL EDUCATION

What's a 'cri de coeur', cunt?

It's French for 'cry from the heart'. A plaintive,
heartfelt plea. Or summat

It's a great line, from that poem

Oh I see, I thought you were asking me a question
and calling me a cunt

Want another drink?

Yeah baby, they'll chisel 'poet' when they do you

ATAVISTIC

The best part of a woman's body is just here
Where your tail used to be
Maybe it's atavistic of me

My father once came across these notebooks I kept
Words I learnt and never used
Words like atavistic
My father was intelligent but conflicted

I think it will take another generation for these
ideas to filter through
For the notebooks to be of use

'

BORIS BIKE

He said he liked to see a girl on a Boris Bike

Disposable

You just chuck it on the floor when you're done
with it

I think I want to be his Boris Bike

BLIND

He knew the name of every bird and which song it
would sing

I knew the song
But never the bird

As if it could have been every bird I had ever
encountered
Together in harmony

I had met every bird
And thought I knew every song as if it were the
same each and every time

I'm coming to learn I will never know every song
Or every bird
No matter how hard I try

MONDAY MORNING REGRET

He arrives early in the morning
Or sometimes round about noon
I don't know if he's been yet
But surely he must come soon

Trash man trash man
I'm sorry I never put my bins out

MY 22nd BIRTHDAY

I spent the day in bed
In my apartment
Rue Bergère

I spent my 22nd birthday
In bed

In the most beautiful city moulded by man
On my birthday

Why did man mould a city so beautiful
For girls who spend the day in bed?

THE LEAF SWEEPER
OF
THE JARDIN DU PALAIS ROYAL

I stroll to the Palais Royal
Every day

I come here in the morning
And in the morning
I see the leaf sweeper

The leaf sweeper of the Jardin du Palais Royal

Because
Each day the leaves fall
Some days more than others
The leaf sweeper turns up
He sweeps the leaves
For there is no bad job

Yet when I turn up
At the Jardin du Palais Royal
Every day
There is nothing waiting for me

I thought every Englishman must be you

If I was the leaf sweeper I'd have a reason to look
down

The leaves fall regardless of you
And I could always be a leaf sweeper